How To Not Fucking Kill Yourself

By Daniel Burton

First Edition, December 2020

ISBN 978-1-716-82554-5

These are poems and they are about my life here.

Silence.

Contents.

Stillness

Sometimes I try really hard and everyone thinks I really love them and I do god damn it but it never holds, it never will. Every love I've had, every friend I've loved, every love I've tossed, that has tossed me.

Why did you toss me? I thought we had the only thing that was real.

It really hurt. I wasn't mad because I didn't understand. I was mad because we were going to protect each other and I got really hurt.

Is none of this real?

I will find a way out.

You Were In Love

If you felt like everything you ever felt, or didn't feel, suddenly made sense, and the years spent in agony, literally agony, crying every night, trying to just leave, leave reality, *LET ME OUT!*, *why the fuck am I here, why the fuck are any of us here?* were worth it now even if you never get another moment of peace, if when the dealer asks if you would rather *all that* or *nothing* you say *that* without a moments hesitation, and even though you literally sit alone now rejecting every element of life, trying to get the strength to kill yourself, you don't because you know the truth, which is that even a memory of that is worth sticking around for, even if you didn't spend any more time together, because there was something that you knew that they knew that was some parts *holy shit* and some parts *how the fuck* and some parts *thank fucking God* and all parts *finally*, and if it's over you know damn well it was what you wanted more than anything else in the world and if it changed everything about you because you used to be agony and regret and now nothing was agonizing and nothing was regrettable, even the worst life you could live for yourself, you were in love.

Winter

Death.

How To Not Fucking Kill Yourself

There is literally never any information. Never anything to actually help. Just a number for a suicide hotline, and a lot of information on why life is so fun, so worth living, god loves; you and the world, and you are here. Don't be sad, you'll regret it.

Stop fucking telling me who to be.

There is never anything that helps. All of that shit just makes me want to kill myself more.

I found my own information. People who are sad, giving directions on how to stay sad, how to be unhappy. *Why not?*

Fuck happy. What about honest?

Did something happen to real?

No, I know we are looking at it backwards. That before this being sad would have been a waste of time, and wasting time was a death wish.

Still... that's not true anymore. So I just went and asked for any information about "How to not fucking kill yourself."

HEEEEEEEEEEEEEEEEEEEEEEEEEEEEEEEEEEEEEEEEEEEEEEEEE
EEEEEEEEEEEEEEEEEEEEEEEEEEEEEEEEEEEEEEEEEEEEEEEEEE
EEEEEEEEEEEEEEEEEEEEEEEEEEEEEEEEEEEEEEEEEEEEEEEEEE
EEEEEEEEEEEEEEEEEEEEEEEEEEEEEEEEEEEEEEEEEEEEEEEEEE
EEEEEEEEEEEEEEEEEEEEEEEEEEEEEEEEEEEEEEEEEEEEEEEEEE
EEEEEEEEEEEEEEEEEEEEEEEEEEEEEEEEEEEEEEEEEEEEEEEEEE
EEEEEEEEEEEEEEEEEEEEEEEEEEEEEEEEEEEEEEEEEEEEEEEEEE
EEEEEEEEEEEEEEEEEEEEEEEEEEEEEEEEEEEEEEEEEEEEEEEEEE
EEEEEEEEEEEEEEEEEEEEEEEEEEEEEEEEEEEEEEEEEEEEEEEEEE
EEEEEEEEEEEEEEEEEEEEEEEEEEEEEEEEEEEEEEEEEEEEEEEEEE
EEEEEEEEEEEEEEEEEEEEEEEEEEEEEEEEEEEEEEEEEEEEEEEEEE
EEEEEEEEEEEEEEEEEEEEEEEEEEEEEEEEEEEEEEEEEEEEEEEEEE
EEEEEEEEEEEEEEEEEEEEEEEEEEEEEEEEEEEEEEEEEEEEEEEEEE
EEEEEEEEEEEEEEEEEEEEEEEEEEEEEEEEEEEEEEEEEEEEEEEEEE
EEEEEEEEEEEEEEEEEEEEEEEEEEEEEEEEEEEEEEEEEEEEEEEEEE
EEEEEEEEEEEEEEEEEEEEEEEEEEEEEEEEEEEEEEEEEEEEEEEEEE
EEEEEEEEEEEEEEEEEEEEEEEEEEEEEEEEEEEEEEEEEEEEEEEEEE
EEEEEEEEEEEEEEEEEEEEEEEEEEEEEEEEEEEEEEEEEEEEEEEEEE
EEEEEEEEEEEEEEEEEEEEEEEEEEEEEEEEEEEEEEEEEEEEEEEEEE
EEEEEEEEEEEEEEEEEEEEEEEEEEEEEEEEEEEEEEEEEEEEEEEEEE
EEEEEEEEEEEEEEEEEEEEEEEEEEEEEEEEEEEEEEEEEEEEEEEEEE
EEEEEEEEEEEEEEEEEEEEEEEEEEEEEEEEEEEEEEEEEEEEEEEEEE
EEEEEEEEEEEEEEEEEEEEEEEEEEEEEEEEEEEEEEEEEEEEEEEEEE
EEEEEEEEEEEEEEEEEEEEEEEEEEEEEEEEEEEEEEEEEEEEEEEEEE
EEEEEEEEEEEEEEEEEEEEEEEEEEEEEEEEEEEEEEEEEEEEEEEEEE
EEEEEEEEEEEEEEEEEEEEEEEEEEEEEEEEEEEEEEEEEEEEEEEEEE
EEEEEEEEEEEEEEEEEEEEEEEEEEEEEEEEEEEEEEEEEEEEEEEEEE
EEEEEEEEEEEEEEEEEEEEEEEEEEEEEEEEEEEEEEEEEEEEEEEEEE
EEEEEEEEEEEEEEEEEEEEEEEEEEEEEEEEEEEEEEEEEEEEEEEEEE
EEEEEEEEEEEEEEEEEEEEEEEEEEEEEEEEEEEEEEEEEEEEEEEEEE
EEEEEEEEEEEEEEEEEEEEEEEEEEEEEEEEEEEEEEEEEEEEEEEEEE
EEEEEEEEEEEEEEEEEEEEEEEEEEEEEEEEEEEEEEEEEEEEEEEEEE
EEEEEEEEEEEEEEEEEEEEEEEEEEEEEEEEEEEEEEEEEEEEEEEEEE
EEEEEEEEEEEEEEEEEEEEEEEEEEEEEEEEEEEEEEEEEEEEEEEEEE
EEEEEEEEEEEEEEEEEEEEEEEEEEEEEEEEEEEEEEEEEEEEEEEEEE
EEEEEEEEEEEEEEEEEEEEEEEEEEEEEEEEEEEEEEEEEEEELP.

I'm sorry.

Last year…

… was a long one.

Anyone?

Don't let the language monster get you it wants to eat your soul I know you are all scared I am not I am but I admit I lost.

Don't let the people get you the language monster is hypnosis.

Did I break the illusion?

If I confused you it got you GET. THE. FUCK. AWAY. but be sneaky it doesn't like people leaving it doesn't like people leaving it doesn't like peo-

Ice Dream

As a child I had this dream. I wake up in the middle of the night in an old cabin, in a metal bed. The walls of the room are a very dark wood, and full of splinters. The Krimstein children, close family friends of mine, are sleeping in the room directly to my right. I don't open their door. I am aware they are in there. I consider going in there with them, but I don't. Theirs is the only door to my right. To my left there extends a long hallway of doors, none of which I know what is behind. They are all facing the same direction as my own. I walk outside. It is snowing. I walk up a hill. I do not know where I am going. I arrive at a cliff, facing back the way I came. I can see the cabin below; the stars above. I am two-hundred feet up into the space in the middle. I jump off, expecting to fall, and to die. Instead I fall impossibly slowly and land face down in the snow.

I lie there, and then I stand up. I climb the hill, reach the cliff, and jump. I fall impossibly slowly and land. I take no damage. I repeat this until I wake up.

I used to have that dream constantly as a child for close to ten years. I have had it more times than I can count.

Sometimes I jump a dozen times, for what feels like hours. Sometimes I wake up before I even hit the ground once. Sometimes I lay in the snow for hours after a fall. Sometimes I have a passion for the work and rise again with a sense of urgency. Sometimes I want to die, because I think if I do this might end. Sometimes I know it will end anyways, and I jump until it does.

The dream stopped when I left my home. I haven't had it since.

I always want to go back there.

Forest

The forest was calm.
A place Hext liked to call home.
It didn't mind him.
Gave him food, game and berries and tubers.
It didn't mind.
It was working on something important. *(Forests always are)*

Only when it rained, did the long, fanning leaves seem to slouch.
Possibly, he thought, *taking a meal.*
Or a nap.

It didn't matter - no mind.

The Leaving

Broken only to rebuild again.
If it all collapses just take my hand.

We'll jump the abyss before we fall in
And float, forever

Just
Below

Heaven.

Blood

I've been feeling fucked up, washed out, a diamond.
I know you think about then.
Question things when I'm sleeping.
No time - just dream: life is too much for me.

Headshot when I talk about my own damn problems.
I'm a cynic, I'm a killer, and I'm so damn obnoxious.
My confidence been fucking wasted on some half-cocked fucks.
I wish I'd saved it for a girl that wouldn't break my heart.

Now I'm too damn crazy?
"Daniel we love you, can we change you?
We just want you to be happy or a goddamn stranger." God damn...

...

That's what I told her.

She's brilliant I guess... More tapped in at her saddest than me at my best,
and I'm not even scratching the surface of how bad I know it can get.
I ain't lost what she's lost.
I wish I could have been her treasure chest.

I thought she was my everything
and I treated her like anything.

After I Die

If I'm wrong, that nothing matters
and the afterlife is what comes after
then I guess death is heavensent
and if not
it's still
irrelevant.

Thoughts

It's really hard to be alive and honest because dying is the most honest thing a human can do. I can't show you but if you watch you'll see. BUT I CAN SAVE THE WORLD! That's not your job. I keep going. I haven't been this lost in a long time (welcome back). There is nobody and nothing that you have to be. Whatever identity you've built for yourself... if you don't like it you can leave it behind any time. Nobody will blame you for being inconsistent. Wanting to kill/fuck everybody is ok. And nobody can tell you not to. Having dark thoughts is human. You can be yourself no matter who's watching. Even if everybody in the entire world is watching you can be a version of yourself you like to see. I was sitting in class thinking about love 。 ° °(⊃≽⌣≼⊂) ° °。 The treasure inside is obvious. The question is how to get it. Who am I? How are you? Time is a distance. My life is not a story, but for some reason I am telling it that way. The question is, if I am telling the story, who is living it? Humanize who you idolize. Kill your gods. I wanted to die and then I found a version of me that wanted to exist and the people beat it out of me until I wanted to die. I feel so fucking alone. But that means I am alive... I know talking will just get me killed. I am trying but I am a human. It doesn't have to be some heroic victory. I just figured if I was a hero then everyone would forgive me. I figured if I was a hero then I could forgive myself... So crazy how many people used to get sad at me for being myself. With love, wherever we are. Exclaim, of the people, a word so loud, long and bright that they who heard it would never cease to listen, never cease to concede confusion, for in the understanding must lie some uncomparable truth, and of course the words meaning has no value, but the meaning lies in the structure of the word itself. I was sitting in class thinking about dying. Pay attention! You're going to be ok. I know everybody has stresses and everybody has hardship but just remember at the end of this you die. People will tell you you have to, but you don't have to believe them. I feel so alone because I am alone. I can fake it just to make it but I don't. If I did can only make it fake, I won't. I really meant this one. It has been really hard to go from being seen as a king to a baby. All I ever asked to be seen as was myself. Hide inside of reality? What if reality hides inside of us? Keep falling. Weekend and summer and winter and die. It was so sad because like literally all of my life was designed so that all anybody who loved me wanted for me was to not feel what I felt. What they think of you doesn't matter but what you think of you actually does so if there's something you don't like about yourself talk to yourself and see what you want to change. Every time I have lived a lie all I have ever done is wasted very, very valuable time. I wish somebody would connect with me, about things I like. I feel so alone, I wish somebody would come talk to me about dying and that the universe really doesn't exist but nobody does they want to pussyfoot around art and if I'm ok. Telling me "it's nice to see a real person under there" is like when people tell girls "you should smile more," just shut the fuck up and let me live my life. I want to yell "THINK!" but I know if you ever would you don't need me to. Where is he? He's there, you just aren't seeing him. IHATETHISIHATET HISIHATETHISIHATETHISIHATETHISIHATETHISIHATETHISIHATE THISIHATETHISIHATETHIS. The Myth is always greater than The Man. People will always tell the story they want to tell about you either way. Just let them do that, focus on who you ARE. No stories. I really want this to end if I have to die for it just hurry up please. I know I go through pain so you can all feel too, but it really hurts. When you're ready, I promise. I was sitting in the hall already dead.

GOD.

DAMN

IT!!!!!!!

Want To Take Tea?

Want to take tea in the parlor room? A man got his head cut off in there.

What about grandmother. That old bitch sucks.

I don't think of old people that way any more.

Does it scare you, that when you are old you will still not know what is going on. That you will be as a child as you are now?

You should learn how to be ok without being ok.

I worry you are all really dumb, and I try to talk to you all, but it always turns out I am dumb, and nobody can save anyone except themself.

Well, at least when I see it my way I do that.

Your way may be more humble though. It makes me sad, but it is more humble. I need to take some lessons.

You Bought It

Ayy
Ayy
Ayy
Ay-

I go to a party I'm a fun guy
That's right just like mushrooms I'm a fun time.
I pop Molly, fuck I feel like I can fly
I don't crash cause I don't got no pain inside.
I can hide forever in the cloudy place
If everybody sees me then I'm super safe
If everybody sees me they don't doubt a thing
If I've got pain I just pretend I'm like a king.

You bought it...

I throw parties nobody will know me now
I can hide with everybody else around
I scream so nobody thinks I make a sound
I open up my mouth none of my words come out.
I don't live a lie the world is just fucked
You would see it but I think you kinda suck
I don't hate nobody that includes myself
Don't look now I fucking want to kill myself.

You bought it...

Dark and stormy nobody picks up the phone.
I feel so alone because I am alone.
I can fake it just to make it but I don't
If I did can only make it fake I won't.
Patience is a gift, I don't like my god.
I like death and she likes me but not alive.
I keep trying to be honest then I die,
Well not quite die but I am lucky to be live.

I don't want my old friends and they don't want me.
I don't have new friends I don't have anything.
I was right I know that's why you never call
I never liked you I don't have hope its all lies.
I don't feel bad I don't have time I just feel
I can't question even though this isn't real.
I still hate myself when I am him not me
I am him right now so right now I hate me...

You bought it.

Nobody

I'm sick of being a vessel
For everyone's distorted fantasies
So when I demand to just be seen
You all light me up with kerosene.

You said it's obscene that I don't care about you,
Or anyone, or me,
Then wake up the next day with a headache.

It's not fair
That you would leave me
To be the only one to carry that memory
It's too heavy and I've already got a lot on my back.

I let you make a million choices, I let you decide alone if we would keep it
But you still played me like I'm clingy when I lied about the visit
And I'm lying on your couch
I've got my own that I'd rather be on
I wasn't there for me
But you still acted like I was.

You just hated and you hurt me
So when I left I didn't look back.

It was easy because I know you never loved me.

It was easy because I know you don't love anyone, not even yourself
The difference between us is you still haven't accepted that.

I can't handle being a villain
I've been one before I was born.

I think my mother wanted to kill me.
I think she always loved me more.

I know she felt the pain but I ask you now where did I get that?

It's not that hard to figure.
It's not that hard to figure.

I hate myself when you all love me
I'll say it a million times.

But you still push me back there
And call and say
"You sound like you're doing well."

I'm not, I already told you
It's a mask behind which I hide
So I can cry forever without you all telling me you don't want me to(o)
'Cause I do
I accept that.

That's why I only like me
He's the only one worth spending time with
And I can't stand
Another soul getting near mine.

It's not a matter of being hurt
It is, but it's more about how childish egos are.

I want to grow up
So just leave me here.

Have fun trying to find out if it was worth it
'Cause it's not that fun but it's worth it since it's the only one.

And that's the answer, don't overthink.

It's not time yet but when it is you'll probably be ready.

Fuck.

Madness curing sadness and of course the inverse is true
When I beat myself up for daydreaming
About things I want
But will never have
It's ok, I'm just erasing futures
For the real one headed my way.

I know so much that God is mad at me.
"Leave it alone" he says,
"I've got a plan."
"Fuck off." is my reply.

We fight, like brothers of a certain age, like brothers who trust each other,
who do not fear each other, or more accurately fear the other who fears
himself.

We fight and he wins.
Who would I be to be able to do otherwise?
And he does not laugh and he does not cry he truly means it when he is
trying to help
"WELL WHY!!" I yell, this time not at the sky.
This time under my own breath. To the inside of my head
Where I know the universe truly is.
"Why like this...?"
"Because I'm God" comes the reply. *"I don't know how else to help you."*

Sadness curing madness
Finally
Finding death, and finding truth,
And she loves me just as much as I thought she did,
And I can't wait to see her soon in the grand scheme of things.

I almost died. Holding on for what could have been dear life. I had never not
had the strength before and this time I didn't and I did not die I knew I
would barely be hurt.

God always tries to speak to me in numbers. 1:11, 2:22, 3:33, 4... well you get the idea.

I, who was waiting for a magic flight, a hero's journey nearly complete, the boon in fucking god damn hand, fell 20 or more feet to a bed of rocks and walked my way out, albeit on a broken foot, of a muddy dried river too deep to have climbed out save for a piece of wood, no other objects in sight, that happened to be laying near my path.

And I, who was screaming, demanding he leave me alone, picked up the wood, not meant to be a ladder but possibly, and used it as such since it was formed almost so.

And when I hit the road I laid on my back and when I asked what to do he said *"Heal or die. Not die, but fight, and you are fighting on behalf of death."*

I called the hospital and in the transport to the ER it occurred to me...
This was the magic flight.
I tried not to laugh, to ground myself in here and now and not get lost in time and space and when I got to the hospital and checked the time as they wheeled me in the fucking clock said it was 4:44 A.M.

(Fuck, it's just hard to be honest and alive when everybody is so... fucking scared)

I Hate…

I hate color, I hate greyscale, I hate people, I hate living
I hate dying, I hate breathing, I hate when people ask me questions.
I hate my dumb cunt of a therapist
I hate when people censor me
I hate you, I hate myself, I hate that you don't care about me.
I hate when people blame me
But they never blame my parents
I hate how dumb you all are
And I hate how if I talk about it I am too.
I hate when women try to fix me.
I hate when women try to fix me.
I hate when gay friends aren't my friends they just want to fuck me.
I hate when people say I'm just pissed off because I won't admit I'm gay
And I hate when they try to fuck me after that.
I hate that people think I'm crazy
I hate that people don't think this is a choice
I hate that I can see the universe
But people just think I'm having a schizophrenic episode or being egotistical
unless I use that ability to help them.
Then they think I am so wise and so special. I hate that.

I hate when people won't just fucking leave me alone
Except when I need help, *then* they leave me alone.
I hate that people call me selfish,
Or say I lack remorse, but they only want me to have remorse
So they can get what *they* want.
I hate you.
I hate this.
I hate.

Ghost

I:
If it was perfect,
I guess it will be
I don't know why we have to go
But I know you
So I don't feel so alone

II:
I know I hide my pain behind my ego
It's a bad side of me to show
And I'm sorry I tried to see you as more than you

III:
And I'm sorry it's taken me so long to learn
Things you've known all along
But I am learning
It's all I do ~

IV:
I want to find you
And do this for you
But we all walk these roads alone
I'm not a god, I'm not a man, I'm just a soul

V:
I see how I'm selfish
I don't mean to hurt
I'm just scared of letting go
I just don't know how to deal with feeling so alone

VI:
And I know there's never anything to say
And I broke the other rule
And its me that's supposed to apologize
I know.

.

How To Finally Enjoy Yourself.

stop.

ok?

CPSIA information can be obtained
at www.ICGtesting.com
Printed in the USA
BVHW082010161121
621782BV00007B/815